BABYSITTING

Babysitting JOBS

THE BUSINESS OF BABYSITTING

by Barbara Mehlman

Consultant: Beth Lapp
Certified Babysitting Training Instructor

Capstone
press®

Mankato, Minnesota

Snap Books are published by Capstone Press,
151 Good Counsel Drive, P.O. Box 669, Mankato, Minnesota 56002.
www.capstonepress.com

Library of Congress Cataloging-in-Publication Data

Mehlman, Barbara.

Babysitting jobs: the business of babysitting / Barbara Mehlman.

p.cm.—(Snap books. Babysitting)

Summary: "A guide for pre-teens and teens on how to get and keep babysitting jobs"—Provided by publisher.

Includes bibliographical references and index.

ISBN-13: 978-0-7368-6463-3 (hardcover)

ISBN-10: 0-7368-6463-6 (hardcover)

1. Babysitting—Vocational guidance—Juvenile literature. 2. Preteens—Employment—Juvenile literature.

I. Title. II. Series.

HQ769.5.M44 2007

649'.10248—dc22   2006001733

Editor: Becky Viaene

Designer: Jennifer Bergstrom

Photo Researcher/Photo Editor: Kelly Garvin

Photo Credits: Barbara Mehlman, 32; Capstone Press/Karon Dubke, cover, 7, 9, 10–11, 12–13, 21, 25; Capstone Press/ TJ Thoraldson Digital Photography, 14–15, 26–27; Corbis/FK PHOTO, 22–23; Corbis/Roy Morsch, 4–5; Corbis/zefa/Emely, 17; Corbis/zefa/K. Solveig, 28; SuperStock/Kwame Zikomo, 18–19

1 2 3 4 5 6 11 10 09 08 07 06

Table of Contents

CHAPTER 1

More Than Just Making Money

You may not be old enough yet to be a waitress or a cashier. But you are the right age to be a babysitter.

Remember when you had a babysitter? You enjoyed when she played board games with you and read you stories. Well, now you can babysit and do all the fun things your sitter did with you. Only this time, you get to be in charge and make money too.

However, babysitting is about more than just making money. It can be a fun and rewarding experience. But this job isn't right for everyone. Before you consider babysitting, ask yourself the following questions:

• Do you enjoy being with children?

• Do you think doing "kid stuff" is fun?

• Do you have time to babysit?

If you answered "yes" to these questions, then you'll probably enjoy babysitting.

This book will help you start your own babysitting business. You'll learn what type of babysitting jobs you want and how to get and keep jobs. Soon you'll be the best babysitter in your neighborhood.

Getting Experience

Before you go out to get your first paying babysitting job, you'll want to get some experience.

Most people are hesitant about hiring someone without babysitting experience. You can prepare for your first job by taking a babysitting training course, volunteering, and getting references.

Get Advice and Training

The American Red Cross offers excellent babysitting and CPR training courses. Your parents also can show you how to change a diaper and feed a baby. Practice changing a diaper on a doll so that you get good at it.

Ask to Volunteer

After you've had training, you can get some experience by volunteering. Offer to babysit your siblings or cousins while parents are home. Ask the parents to observe you and suggest helpful hints.

Ask for References

Once you have some experience babysitting, ask parents for references. References are letters saying that parents think you are a good babysitter and would recommend you. The more references and experience you have, the easier it will be to get a babysitting job.

CHAPTER 3

How to Get Hired

After you have babysitting training, experience, and references, it's time to get some real paying jobs. But how do you find families that need a babysitter?

O ne of the best ways to get paying jobs is to advertise. You can make attractive advertising flyers to post on public bulletin boards. Put up your flyers at the library, places of worship, grocery stores, and other places where parents shop. Check out the tips on the next page and get ready to advertise!

Babysitter

555 – 7237

Tips For Making Babysitting Flyers

* If you create your flyers by hand, make sure they are neat. Use a ruler and a pencil to draw light guidelines so your writing is straight.

* Make the flyers colorful, but don't use yellow in the lettering because it's hard to read.

* List the times you're available.

* Include your phone number.

* List your name and number many times at the bottom of each flyer so parents can tear it off without taking the flyers.

CHAPTER 4

Making a Good Impression

A few weeks after posting babysitting flyers you may receive some calls. Now it's time to meet the interested families. You feel excited and nervous.

Try not to be nervous about making a good first impression. It's as easy as smiling, shaking hands, and showing that you're a warm and friendly person. It's a good idea to practice shaking hands with someone. Giving a firm handshake shows confidence.

But smiling and a handshake alone won't get you the job. You will also need to look nice. Skip wearing your torn jeans. Instead, wear something conservative, such as a sweater and clean jeans.

Parents will likely ask you questions about your babysitting experience. Being prepared with examples of how you've handled babysitting situations is a great way to make a good impression.

QUESTIONS TO ASK BEFORE ACCEPTING A BABYSITTING JOB

Parents shouldn't be the only ones asking questions. Find out:

* How many children will I be watching?
* Do the children have any disabilities?
* Will I be paid by the hour or per child?

Resumes and References

When you meet a client for the first time, bring your resume and references. Your resume should have information about your babysitting experience, like when you began babysitting. Your resume will likely include babysitting for family members and volunteering.

Not sure what to include on a resume? Use the example on page 13 as a guide.

Jane Doe
Babysitter

Contact:
22 Sycamore Street
Oakwood, New York 10006
Phone: 555-100-1000
Email: jdoe@anyplace.com

Available:
Monday-Thursday 5 p.m.-7 p.m.
Friday 3 p.m.-1 a.m.

Clients

Sarah and Steve Smith
Phone: 555-5555
Experience: I've babysat the Smiths' two daughters since January. They are ages two and four.

John and Ashley Olson
Phone: 555-4444
Experience: I've babysat the Olsons' son since March. He is age seven.

Education

School: Hoover High School
Phone: 555-1122
Counselor: Mrs. Nelson
Grade: 9

Training

I have completed the American Red Cross babysitting training course and a first aid training class.

Interest:

I enjoy reading, playing the clarinet, and playing basketball.

CHAPTER 5

Tips for Keeping Jobs

Hooray! You did it! You landed your first real paying job. Now what?

Now you want to make sure the parents hire you again. Many qualities and skills make someone a good babysitter. To get an excellent start for the job, be on time. If you think you might be late, call the parents.

What Good Babysitters Do

Another important part of being a good babysitter is knowing about child development and age-appropriate activities. Come prepared with books and games to entertain the children.

Good babysitters also let parents know what happens while they're gone. Tell parents what and when the children ate, and when they went to bed. Make sure that everything you say is true.

Helpful Hint

Send a note to parents to let them know how much you enjoyed being with their children and that you would like to sit for them again.

What Good Babysitters Don't Do

Good babysitters also know what not to do. Some things, such as letting kids jump on furniture, are obviously wrong.

Good babysitters don't talk on the phone all evening or invite friends over. They know that their main job is to keep the kids safe and entertained.

Most importantly, good babysitters don't break the house rules or snoop through the family's personal belongings. A good rule is to not do anything while parents are gone that you wouldn't be comfortable doing right in front of them.

WHAT WOULD YOU DO?
Your favorite TV show is on during the time when you're babysitting. You really want to watch it.

SIMPLE SOLUTION
Don't watch the show while you're supposed to be watching the kids. You could record the show and watch it later. Or next time pass on babysitting so you can watch the show.

Job Decisions

You might not feel comfortable watching babies yet. Or you think babysitting more than two kids at a time feels like too many.

It's OK to politely turn down job offers that aren't right for you. You should only take jobs you're comfortable with.

Whether you just started babysitting or you've been babysitting for years, answer the questions on the next few pages. They'll give you a better idea of what types of babysitting jobs are right for you.

How many children do you think you can handle?

Caring for two or more children can be difficult. It's OK if you only feel comfortable babysitting one child.

What age children do you prefer to babysit?

You may enjoy watching kids of all ages. If you have a favorite age, it's OK to be honest. You may only want to watch older children, especially when you start babysitting.

Are you willing to babysit difficult children?

Some children are challenging to watch. They may refuse to go to sleep or cry a lot. Babysitting difficult children requires more skill. If you agree to watch a difficult child, you must be very patient.

What days and times are you available for babysitting?

Only take a job if you have enough time. Be sure you set aside time to do your homework, help around the house, and spend time with friends. It's not fair to do homework or watch TV on the job when you should be playing with the children.

REASONS TO TURN DOWN A JOB

You likely won't be able to babysit every time someone asks. Sometimes even when you can babysit, you may not want to. Here are a few good reasons for turning down jobs.

* You or one of the children is sick.
* You have to study for a big test. Schoolwork should always come first.
* You feel uncomfortable babysitting for the family.

How do you feel about babysitting for families that are different from yours?

Families are different in many ways, from religion to the food they eat. You may be amazed how different other families are from yours. Don't accept a babysitting job unless you can respect the differences while you babysit.

Do you have a ride to and from your client's house?

Make sure you have someone to take you to your job and bring you home. Usually the parents of the children you'll be watching will take care of this.

CHAPTER 7

Getting Paid

You can avoid awkward situations by discussing payment before you accept a babysitting job.

Talk with parents about whether you'll be paid by the hour or per child. Decide if you'll charge the same for each family. Make sure you don't charge too much, or you'll price yourself out of a job.

When you begin babysitting, you may not know what is a fair rate to charge. You can find out the going rate by asking your friends how much they get paid. Also, ask other parents how much they pay their babysitters.

WHAT WOULD YOU DO?
The children's parents drop you home and say they'll pay you next time.

SiMPLE SOLUTiON
The next time you babysit for the family it's OK to remind them about the payment. But don't argue with them about it. If they refuse to pay you, stop sitting for them.

Expanding Your Business

Once you've been babysitting for a while, you'll gain experience and confidence. But how do you turn an occasional night of babysitting into a regular job?

One of the best ways to earn more money is to babysit for families that need a sitter each week. You can also expand your business by offering to babysit for more than one family at a time. If you know that one of your clients is going out with another couple, offer to watch their children too. During summer, when you're on break from school, you can offer to do full-day babysitting. As you get older, you may even decide to babysit full-time all summer as a nanny.

Referrals

Another way to expand your babysitting business is to ask your parents and families you've babysat for to refer you to their friends. You can also ask people you know well, like your teachers, to refer you. After all, they know how responsible you are. Don't forget to ask your friends if you can be their substitute in case they have to cancel. The word will quickly spread that you are a good babysitter. Soon you'll have so many jobs that you may even have to turn some down.

Jane Doe
Babysitter

Available:
Monday-Thursday 5 p.m.-7 p.m.
Friday 3 p.m.-1 a.m.

I have completed the American
Red Cross babysitting training
course and a first aid training class.

555-100-1000
jdoe@anyplace.com

BUSINESS CARDS

When you're asking parents to refer you, make sure you have a business card to give them. On the card make sure to include:

* Your name and telephone number
* Days and times when you're available to babysit
* Training you have completed (especially CPR and babysitting training courses)

Time to Work!

From making flyers to getting experience, you're ready to enter the world of babysitting. You now know how to overcome one of the toughest parts of babysitting–getting jobs. So get ready to work. It's time to start one of the most rewarding jobs you may ever have.

Checklist:

Are You Ready For a Babysitting Job?

You can't wait to start babysitting. But are you really ready for the job? Answer these questions to find out.

✓ Do you have experience? If not, get some by volunteering.

✓ Have you taken babysitting and CPR training courses?

✓ Do you have a babysitting resume and references?

✓ Have you made a flyer that lists your contact information and experience?

✓ Have you posted flyers to let parents know you're available to babysit?

✓ Do you know what type of babysitting job you want and can handle?

✓ Before accepting a job, did you discuss expectations and payment?

✓ Do you know what things a good babysitter should and shouldn't do if she wants to be asked back?

Glossary

client (KLYE-uhnt)—a person who hires someone to do a job; the parents who hire you to care for their children are your clients.

going rate (GOH-ing RAYT)—the amount most people get for doing a job; babysitters are usually paid a certain amount per hour.

nanny (NAN-ee)—someone who takes care of young children full-time in the children's homes

reference (REF-uh-renss)—a written statement from an employer about a job seeker's character and abilities

resume (RE-zuh-may)—a brief listing of all the jobs, education, and qualifications a person has

Quick Tips

* Sometimes children get asthma or allergy attacks. Take a CPR course, so you'll be prepared. You could save a child's life some day.

* Babies often put strange things in their mouths. They may start choking. Learn the Heimlich maneuver for children and babies.

* Learn first aid. The American Red Cross offers basic first aid training.

* Bring an adult with you when you meet a new client for the first time.

* If you don't already have a bank account, open one just in case clients pay you by check.

Read More

Brown, Harriet. *The Babysitter's Handbook: The Care and Keeping of Kids.* Middleton, Wis.: Pleasant Company, 1999.

Dayee, Frances S. *Babysitting.* New York: Franklin Watts, 2000.

Fine, Jil. *Baby-sitting Smarts.* Smarts. New York: Children's Press, 2002.

Zakarin, Debra Mostow. *The Ultimate Baby-sitter's Handbook: So You Wanna Make Tons of Money?* Los Angeles: Price Stem Sloan, 1997.

Internet Sites

FactHound offers a safe, fun way to find Internet sites related to this book. All of the sites on FactHound have been researched by our staff.

Here's how:

1. Visit *www.facthound.com*

2. Choose your grade level.

3. Type in this book ID **0736864636** for age-appropriate sites. You may also browse subjects by clicking on letters, or by clicking on pictures and words.

4. Click on the **Fetch It** button.

Facthound will fetch the best sites for you!

About the Author

Barbara Mehlman began babysitting at about 10 years old when her new baby brother was born. She continued to babysit all through high school and college to earn extra money until she married and had two lovely daughters of her own.

Now she's a high school librarian and writes a weekly newspaper column on theater. In her spare time, she uses all the babysitting skills she writes about when she takes care of her four young grandchildren, whom she adores.

Index